haha

Paperback ISBN: 978-1-9999309-8-1
eBook ISBN: 978-1-9999309-2-9

haha

Wilson Oryema

CONTENTS

haha

This is another book about Consumption…

haha

and its far-reaching effects.

Introduction

This is a book of poetry about consumption and how things can and will consume us. Some of these include: stress, trauma, addiction, shame, aggression, and grief. These themes will be explored through the lives of the many characters and tales expressed in the following pages. Enjoy.

The tumultuous life of [redacted].

There are certain things you need to feel for yourself. There are also things you should avoid at all costs.

I miss you
The shy
The mild mannered you
The you who stayed at home playing video games
But barely slept or cared for food

I miss you
The vulgar
The aggressive you
The you who had nothing to lose
But in turn had nothing to gain
Apart from short term success
And an infamous name

I miss you
The timid
The frightened you
The you who flinched at the sign of violence
And cried when things didn't go your way

I miss you
I miss it all
The you of yesterday
The you of yesteryear
But to reminisce is not to say things right now are amiss
But to appreciate and show value to why we exist

I find it hard telling the time
When to stay
When to leave

The dreams we tie ourselves to
But never move towards
The places we despise and speak ill of
But never escape from
Or rather
That we never plan to separate from

I find myself stuck in the mud
With a joystick to hand
Slowly sinking
But still playing
Sinking further
No contesting

Someone told me mud baths were good for the body
But may not satisfy as nourishment for the soul

I'm a lot more fragile
Than it seems.

But you'll never hear a squeal
Or a scream.

This mask has been here for 12
And we still have many years to go

Why would I tell someone about it?

— can they help !?

Although I have tossed many coins into the wishing well
It feels like none of mine ever made it to the water

Back when mother woke me up
To rush to school
I was a bitter fool
Cursing my luck and all

If we were clean slates
Every day felt like someone
Just peed in my pool
Or left a lump of stool
Or maybe worse
I cannot recall

Balling up my fists
Swinging at innocent walls
Leaving my knuckles
Bruised, scarred, and deformed

And when that couldn't help
I spent my nights
Screaming into headsets
Arguing about many things
But not a single one
I can remember

The anger ruffles feathers
Ripples along the skin

A snarling wave
Not all tides which
Reach the sand
Are spurned by the beach

Some islands are swallowed
Like the sugar in my tea
Not a grain of sand in sight
Let alone a beach

In the same way
Aggression will rise from your soul
Boiling your bones
And blanketing your skin
In a malicious tone

A colour
Which you may not see
While one uncontrollably seethes
And is eventually
Brought to ruin
By ignoring the soul bleed

Eyes closed
I lost sight of what I had to
Feet bleeding
I ran away from it all
I kept my knees and head to the floor
Hoping
Praying it all changed
Despite not believing in any of the old ways.

Arms extended out the window
Hoping for a beam of light
To drive by and take me away
From this decaying
Smelly old life

The greys
The kobolds
Yoda and Mace Windu
Annu
Spock
The shapeshifters too
Any story
Any culture
I'm just hoping for one to be true

My confidence drops from every eye set upon me
From the soft glances
To the hard stares

Even in the black of night
There seems to be no respite
My dilated eyes can see everything within a square mile

Even in the daytime
Where i should be all smiles
I avoid all contact
Like a confused child in the glass aisle

And I always use the same excuse
"i have to go, sorry"
And hope there's a bus near

Really and truly i have no where I need to be
But the truth is
I'm quite scared

Of what
I definitely wouldn't tell you
Or who
If i gave a hint
You might probably be able to tell too

And why
I have to go sorry, I need to catch a bus to...

Somewhere near the edge

slowly stumbling around
slight bumps may bring me to the ground

Nobody told me I was bleeding
Still flowing
And now it's covering the cement
Should i slip
Who would help
Surely someone decent?

But alas
The weak
And vulnerable
Are rarely in anyone's thoughts

— Stiff upper lip. Stand tall.

I picked and scratched
At the scars and scabs
In hopes that they'll disappear
And never come back

I cannot say where I learned
To persistently scratch
But the "lighter" attacks
In fact worsened
What i had

— we need mandatory classes on self care

Excuse me
Put it away
Please
To entangle those
Closest to you
Is not what
They need
Nor will this
Fare you well
In the end
This may sound
Self-righteous
Plus fear and
Anger may have you
On edge
But take a step
Back
While you still can
Or else…

There
Are
Many
Silent Wars
Going
On
In
The
Same
Places
You
Frequent
And
Pass by
Every
Day

.

— Can what doesn't seemingly concern me, effect me?

I behave in confusing ways
I overcompensate
I dilly dally on beneficial decisions
I am never not late

My ability to prostate and show humility
Seems to be side effect that I cannot escape
Of what... I imagine it to be inadequacy
But society favours the meek so I may choose not to discard my
way to behave
But can it ever be so easy to part ways with the things that made
us who we are today?

After many years of life. I've finally realised I hate myself

I'm sorry. I'm sorry. I'm sorry. I'm sorry. I'm sorry. I'm sorry.
I'm sorry. I'm sorry. I'm sorry. I'm sorry. I'm sorry. I'm sorry.
I'm sorry. I'm sorry. I'm sorry. I'm sorry. I'm sorry. I'm sorry.
I'm sorry. I'm sorry. I'm sorry. I'm sorry. I'm sorry. I'm sorry.
I'm sorry. I'm sorry. I'm sorry. I'm sorry. I'm sorry. I'm sorry.
I'm sorry. I'm sorry. I'm sorry. I'm sorry. I'm sorry. I'm sorry.
I'm sorry. I'm sorry. I'm sorry. I'm sorry. I'm sorry. I'm sorry.
I'm sorry. I'm sorry. I'm sorry. I'm sorry. I'm sorry. I'm sorry.
I'm sorry. I'm sorry. I'm sorry. I'm sorry. I'm sorry. I'm sorry.
I'm sorry. I'm sorry. I'm sorry. I'm sorry. I'm sorry. I'm sorry.
I'm sorry. I'm sorry. I'm sorry. I'm sorry. I'm sorry. I'm sorry.
I'm sorry. I'm sorry. I'm sorry. I'm sorry. I'm sorry. I'm sorry.
I'm sorry. I'm sorry. I'm sorry. I'm sorry. I'm sorry. I'm sorry.
I'm sorry. I'm sorry. I'm sorry. I'm sorry. I'm sorry. I'm sorry.
I'm sorry. I'm sorry. I'm sorry. I'm sorry. I'm sorry. I'm sorry.
I'm sorry. I'm sorry. I'm sorry. I'm sorry. I'm sorry. I'm sorry.
I'm sorry. I'm sorry. I'm sorry. I'm sorry. I'm sorry. I'm sorry.
I'm sorry. I'm sorry. I'm sorry. I'm sorry. I'm sorry. I'm sorry.
I'm sorry. I'm sorry. I'm sorry. I'm sorry. I'm sorry. I'm sorry.
I'm sorry. I'm sorry. I'm sorry. I'm sorry. I'm sorry. I'm sorry.
I'm sorry. I'm sorry. I'm sorry. I'm sorry. I'm sorry. I'm sorry.
Please forgive me. I'm sorry.

The mirror your partner will shine on you
is unforgivingly clear and wide
all your worst aspects
out in the open
things you would never confront
squaring up and trying to catch your fade
while lighting various fires across the garden path
you and your chosen one have made

"You don't wanna know what I've been going through today"

— a message I left for you, it seems you took yourself away to hide from this issue too

Isolation is one of
the most painful things
you can experience
Self-imposed or otherwise.
Related to work or other ties.

I thought of my all my friends,
and called my only one.

We spoke
Pain
Pressure
And the people we lost on the way.

She was in a cemetery
walking the dog.

We were interrupted

The dog pooped on a grave
But she had no doggy bag to take it away

We both laughed

As it may be a metaphor for the messes we make

Hoping
Praying
Someone will take it all away

— Birds of a feather

There are many who glide into our lives
with bright eyes and smiles
Who promise us nebulae
and companionship on this path,
Some follow you all the way and flowers
bloom where you played
Others let you lead
To intercept the cracks along the way
They also exit where they may

— Find your allies

You can eat excessively to cover it up.
You can drink till you pass out and forget.
You can can buy 100 new clothes in case your insecurities show.
You can get on the first train to a far away place to run from a problem you don't want to face.
You can wear a mask to hide your shame.
You can repeat all these things till you're blue in the face or the colour goes away
But it doesn't mean you will ever escape them.

— Address them

Can you curb your addictions
Should you curb your addictions
My addictions keep me sane
My addictions keep me tamed
I'm not sure what i would be without them

"My withdrawals taught me love"

As a younger man
I was consumed by the distractions

The Blinding lights
The Numbing sounds

My affections created a burning hole in my pockets
And probably my retinas

No fire extinguisher
No wet towel to pat it down

And halting my desires
Was something i wouldn't allow

So as i slept on my burning mound
I dreamt of unhindered opulence

Instead i awoke to the strong smell of smoke
The fire left me stark and exposed

Which no tears could wash away
It seemed the fire would not be kept at bay

But guess what... I made it here today

Swimming from all my problems

My problems left me in a cesspool
Filled with fear, self-loathing, and a strong mix of cocktails

Any hopes of floating to the surface
Negated by downward currents of
Negronis, Daiquiris, Margaritas, and Martinis

Inaction meant more was added to the pool
With chalky reds and Smooth whites in tow

— The weight of my vices may drag me down to hell

The fish out of water flops about out of desperation

Rapidly
The Hands & Heart
Shake
I cannot contain

I longed for a budding connection
Instead felt instantaneous burn and unexpected separation

And yet, it's only been a few moments

— Ha!

More spew on my pillow
blood again
Dribble on my clothes
Phlegm in the sink

I fall asleep
I awake
Cycles repeat

Take some water
Look at my phone
I stay awake in the hopes
That I won't cough up a stream

The demons are here for the summer
With baggies and bottomless drinks for our pleasure

Chew, lick, bite, sniff, gulp
Then more of the same

Curtains drawn in lowly rooms
I have yet to find a better place to hide my shame

My demons are still here for the summer
Falling in and out of cars
Picking up
Falling in and out of cabs
Throwing up
A glorious soup of ups, downs, love
And whatever else we could grasp in our clutch

With no end in sight
I close my eyes
But more demons have arrived
To keep both ends of my candle alight

I wonder
How long can this continue
How long can I carry on

The further you look into the abyss
The further you are from making it out

— Light louts

Where do you want to be at 65?

— Hopefully Alive

I continue to run the path of pleasure with both arms extended
No destination
No rest points or stations
Picking up whatever extends the trip
letting go of whatever is far too bland to hit

I bathed in my shame
A soup of barbarism and tears if you will
Stewed in it
Unmoving
Uncaring

I've been playing it back in my mind
For the last few months now
The raspy voices
The tear filled tissues
Remnants of a one sided shouting match
I never accepted my invitation to

To live with desire
Is to live in suffering
I can't remember who relayed that
But i feel it to be partly true
Primarily where others feel it necessary to intrude

I just wanted to eat my cake
With no obligations
As was agreed when chose to share a plate
Supposedly even that was too much
And now I'm jumping through hoops to appease you
As if this were a game of double dutch

But as easily as I stepped in
I can easily step out
And hop, skip, step, flip my way onto other tables to enjoy my
fill of cake
Until for them too
it is also enough
And they begin to start acting like you

— sacrifices

Why won't you have cake with me?

haha

"This'll be the last time... I promise"

Like a rollercoaster in the dark
Sharp turns
Steep drops
Beware
It's like a child trying to escape their cot
What gave them comfort
Is now their biggest crutch
And not something one can easily escape from
You may climb out of your baby cage
Thinking safe
Positive thoughts
And fall right into the Lion's den
With no Daniel to support

— Withdrawals

Getting sight of oneself in a mirror

"This is the last time"
"Never again"

Uttered so often it feels like a ritual

Do you tell yourself the truth all the time?

Only if it makes me feel good
Only if it keeps me at peace

— Ignorance is bliss or some other age old idioms would suffice

Searching for the next party
Searching for the next chase
Maybe three drinks or more
Or something else to smooth my pace
This long and lonely road
Has varying bumps all over it
Some we can medicate away
Others we just can't take away
Still
We try to hide them all the same

Hunger strikes of the worst kind
Hoping for an embrace

Hold me close
I'm cold
Give me solace
I'm lost

You can run until your feet bleed
You can run until they turn blue

Close your eyes
Take a chew

Too stringent
Too careless

Your hopes will not come true while you experience the world
through a distorted hue

I thought about my death at one point
every two hours
Like a dry towel after a cold shower
Hoping for a warming embrace
Third time is a charm
Maybe it will bring me forth to a better place

This uncomfortable pain in my stomach won't be flushed away
The smell is somewhat sickly
Self pity
No bathing
And rotting food in the corner

— It went on so long I almost lost all my shame

I wake from my sleep
With another type of searing pain
It seems there are many today
Some from lack of self restraint
Charge that to the game
Compose myself in the day
And get ready for tonight
To go again

While some pain comes from my mates
And manifests in different ways
But none could possibly be my fault
Imagine the shame
I can't be the one for all
As all wont be for one

Imagine consistently letting go of everything you love because
they're all crazy
And no one cares for you the same

— I hope you don't feel this pain

"If everybody's crazy, you're the one that's insane"

The stories we weave
about that which relieves
leaves many to climb unnecessary trees
In hopes of things
that help
our dreams
but in fact deceive
leaving that
and which we hope to achieve
separated by much more than a few feet

Friends who i play only in shallow waters with are usually the ones that trouble me the most

Push me off the edge
And yet they'll ask me

"Why did you do it to yourself?"

At first i thought it was just the *** killing me and making me paranoid. In fact, just as potent, was the ideas attached to it, and what i thought they will think of me.

— Social stigmas will kill us

REALLY… you should try it

"I am never doing that again!"

There's someone I often talk to
And they always complain
That I never show them a clear picture
Or let them into the frame

And I wonder what bothers them

Is it the transparency
Or maybe
I am too opaque for them to see
Maybe
It is the worry something unexpected might be going on beyond
what they see
But alas
There is no grand illusion
I am all you will see.

— I could be living extremely well, or, well… extremely

At times i might slip and break
At times I might suffer
But I can still piece myself together

At times I might want to do worse
To myself
For what reason?
The answer may vary
As I go through the 4 seasons
In time shorter than a weekend

In mind
It's torment
But vocally
I'm not speaking

The laugh lines are being lifted from my face
Internally I'm bleeding

I would put an end to it all
But honestly speaking
I love you too much that I would never want to worry you

I often play it cool
But i feel slightly deranged
I act like water
In the face of your wishy-washy statements

One day it would be mutual gratification
The other day you want the world

One time you told me your fears
And the reason you want to run away
I told you
I'm fine
Take your time
As i'm stuck in place
But even if I weren't
I wouldn't move a trace

But honestly
I'm scared

I catch myself about to scream
In my quiet place
The one you will never see on screen

But through all the pain
I still see clearly
I will never be that vulnerable
I could never be that vulnerable

I AM AT THE EDGE

I feel like a whack-a-mole
both the player and the machine

for you
my emotions completely exposed
with nowhere to hide

and if you don't respond
i feel cold
somehow left alone

i react
i hammer them in

and then
the emotions
shift
from you
to them

i dive in intensely
repeat the whole process

and then
the emotions
shift
from you
to them

and with no way of containing

the game of whack a mole
will seemingly never end

Hold your tongue
Never spew in rage
Vultures make easy work
Of those who offer themselves on a plate

Your little lies
Have built up like
Autumn leaves on a deserted street
And no one cares to clean them up
Not me
Not them

You seem ill equipped
No broom or brush
No special gloves or vacuum suck

But you have your gift
Of gab
And self deprecating
Faux desperate tone
For which i have believed
Far too long

So for now i will say so long
I pray you stay strong
Until you find another
To jump through hoops
And piggyback you through the throng
Although I may smile and play it safe
It hurts and i'm tempted to call it a day

Hold my head
Protect my face

But my tears don't fall
Regardless of time or place

Still writing until my pen falls off the page
To keep those feelings safe
If left inside me they may wither away

"A lie needs a good memory"

Another head knock
Another love lost
Another day but the same troubles hold me tight in a headlock
My brother said
"For what has been lost, there is much to gain"
But the message never mentioned the pain
The abandonment
The sorrow of it all

I was astonished
But now my feelings
Are hidden within mountain high brick walls
With no windows for them to climb out
Or for someone to climb in

— this isn't a cry for help, but please, if you can, light a candle
for me, so I can see my way through the River Styx

I've been seeing no one
So no one could let me down
Or see me close

A child's birth can be compared to a clear summers day
A sun rising out of the shade
Spotless
Not opaque in any way
But at some point in the day
Clouds will gather
Eventually you get your first drop of rain
One could equate it to the first feeling of shame
And of course
Like the rain
It's very unlikely the first spatter of it ever ends the tale
These drops will fall in the thousands
Before the end of your days
Some will hurt more than others
And this shame
Will lead you to cover your face
And constantly lie
To supposedly protect yourself
Because such is the human way
But I am here to show you
The truth hurts
But not as much as the lies may
Which will weigh on your soul
Almost like
One carrying the world on their own

Things seem much worse when keeping a low gaze

— keep your head up

There is not much I thought I could do to fight the shame
It robbed me of all senses
And left me with only excruciating pain
Screaming out into the darkness
Wide smiles and wider sunglasses
Just to cover the strain
Pretending everything was more than ok
That my life couldn't be better in any way
But really
I was thinking
It could've been better to end it any day
Jumping in front of a train
Laying under a bus before it drives away
Strangling myself
Or maybe never waking up again
And six million other ways
To end it

I've been running at a thousand miles an hour
No respite
No time for a shower
Trying to dodge downpour
But flash floods can make light of one
And swallow them whole

Stubbed my toe
Stepped on a sharp tool
Fell down the stairs at age two
Took more knocks to my knee
Than I'd like to
I can barely walk without feeling pain
Stomach pains and all I can think is "ah we're here again"
I injured most parts of my hand playing basketball but every
other day I go back to play
I have difficulty breathing but this sore throat feels like it's about
to go away
Oh
No
Wait
Here it comes again

The phantom aches
We all seem to suffer from
But somehow avoid bringing up

Or maybe that's just me

I may never tell a soul
Some would look upon as vulnerable

But if I fear such
Maybe I am already quite weak

So who knows what the future may hold for me
Some say it isn't ours to see
And what they don't know can't be seen

— Que sera sera

There is something at hand
I can smell it
Even taste it
Like a wet index
Passing my parched lips
The flavour of deceit
Is all too sweet
Especially
When inflicted upon oneself

I imagined this to be harder
Of course thoughts still linger
But rather than painful memories
It's more akin to
Please don't message me
And if you call me
I will simply express to thee
My trust in thee
Has been swept from me
And these winds of fate
Have taken them
To a faraway place
Beyond the mountains and seas
To a place
You will honestly never reach
And you may hold disdain
Plus place the blame on me
Sure
I can bear it all
But just leave me be

Fooled me once
Fooled me twice
It won't happen thrice

— Goodbye

Like a thief in the night
The rage will rob you
Of your treasures
Memories and Guilty pleasures
Friends and some family members
Leaving you
Stumbling through the dark
In search of your loved ones
And possessions
But alas
The thief has gone
Off to consume another
Who has been
Consumed by their aggression

If you slip and fall
Become a bouncing ball

There is a picture
That never leaves my mind
It was there the day I was born

I dream of it every so often

Sometimes it finds me
When the smell of "real life" becomes all too rotten

Sometimes it finds me
Without a care in the world
As you hear me now

But often I cannot see it
I go in search
It smooth evades

From the corner of my eye
Just over my shoulder and behind my ear
I feel it on the nape of my neck
It's a few steps back...

— The thing you are running from is what you end up chasing

I come from a TV generation
Always in anticipation of the next scene
As if our whole life was on display

Thinking that this time…
No, this time…
No, actually, this time…
Is when they jump out and catch me in the act

and you may wonder to yourself
what were they doing
To have themselves constantly on the edge of their seats

But
Lo and behold
There you find them
Waiting for the next scene

Have you ever been traumatised?
If so
When?
Does it still trouble you?
How do you cope?

I had difficulty focusing and chronic self doubt

Are you deflecting?
Because sometimes I do with a quick witted mouth

Sometimes the trauma
Bowls us over in one fell swoop
Then it takes us time to regather the pins
And stand them up too
Typically this is acute
The chronic type is repetitive and occurs over time
Like placing straws on a camel's back
But
If left alone
You never know which one
Might just break the camel's back

Dying of thirst
Somewhere far out in a desert
Would you rather
A mirage
Or see nothing illusory in your presence
The parent you know who is never there
Or the parent who is always present
But never cares
The one who appeared sparingly at good times
But always does well to keep a distance
Or the one
Who keeps you in good tidings
Mostly as a bragging tool for their siblings

At what point
Could a child make these observations
And not be effected?
Who knows?
As although positives can occasionally gleam
Physical and emotional withdrawal
Leave stains on the soul
Almost impossible to clean

"It is easy to develop a large picture when you're focused on the negatives."

Yet another fray
Yet another reason
I cannot run away
To cower is to lose
So one must reject the pain
Constant neglect
Is an expectation I have so long sustained
Tourettes of the verbal and physical kind
Battered my skin
Like fist sized hailstones
On an unprotected terrain
But now they praise my steely demeanour
As it hardened to the pain
Meanwhile
Inside I can hardly feel a thing
Except for
Occasional blinding rage
Or panic signals
Every second of the day

Again again
I seek songs of praise for my worldly gains
The hardened exterior
Ability to minimise pain
But again
It masks my inner disarray
And yet
Still
I can hardly feel a thing
The inanimate objects I've accrued
Are better placed to tell my truths
As I
In freefall
Am torn apart
Pierced by lovers past
Slipping through safety nets
And unable to grasp a branch
Unfortunately it gets deeper
As I cannot reach for a ceiling
Or place my feet on the floor
So standing up for oneself
Isn't possible anymore
Though I doubt it ever was
As I have never
Felt secure
In any way
Shape
Or form

I cannot tell what this is
It's not a scratch
It's not a broken rib
I cannot tell what this is
It's not acute
It's not something I can itch
I cannot tell what this is
It keeps me distracted
It keeps me stiff
Sat in a chair
Ignoring physical needs
Until its time to sleep
Then I wake up
Then I repeat
I cannot tell what this is
Nor where it came from
Was it self inflicted
And if it is something I can escape from

— Alexithymia?

She said the trauma strips us
Of purpose and our only motivations
Although
These things can later resurface
Through escapism or an immersive vocation

Here we are again
The same tale
The same end
Maybe a slightly funnier circumstance
Maybe scarier at the tail end
This time.

How many more spins of the merry-go-round will it take to get?
How many more times will I say yes?
How many more nights can I run through?
How many more times of going through the same repetitive
things would you suggest?

— I'm tired

I bid thee farewell
As I traverse
Further down this path
Not dissimilar to a disused train line
As I may occasionally
Catch a few rocks in my shoes
Dance with some voracious shrews
Perk my ear up
To listen for any trains on the move
And purposely touch the third rail
From time to time
As I don't think
Life is one worth living
If it is only ever smooth
So
With that
I leave you with this tome of truths
Which
I will probably never return to
But
To you
I hope brings some value
Adieu.

haha

Thank you for reading!

ABOUT THE WRITER

Wilson Oryema is based in London, England. He works across various mediums including, photography, text, and film. His works primarily explore human consumption and its effects on the planet.

You can find more of his work at;
www.wilsonoryema.com

www.ingramcontent.com/pod-product-compliance
Lightning Source LLC
Chambersburg PA
CBHW032046040426
42449CB00007B/1011